"It's hard to speak honestly, straightforwardly about rape, incest, alcoholism and other kinds of abuse. We'd all rather not hear about it. We'd rather pretend such things don't exist. **On Our Way...** confronts this difficulty directly and in the voices of those who have been abused. Men, especially, should read this book."

David Budbill
Poet and Playwright

"**On Our Way...** is raw, beautiful, and painfully real. The book tells us in no uncertain terms: this is what abuse and sexual abuse are all about. This is the impact of abuse, its lasting legacy. All of us need to listen to these important words, which are told with such powerful grace and conviction.

I celebrate that these particular voices—many of whom are young teens—have had the courage to stand up to be our teachers."

Marjorie Ryerson
Editorial Director, Safer Society Press

"Founded under the visionary direction of Tracy Penfield, SafeArt's programs and now this moving SafeArt anthology reflect a healing timeline for humanity.

By unlocking memories and revealing the pain of past relationships, then sharing with others in the present moment through creative, constructive works of art, the possibility returns for a healed future, an evolution of heart. SafeArt participants re-imagine a world where compassion and creativity lie at the core of all our relationships and our humanity."

Lyn Dalebout
Poet

"As exemplified in this anthology, the work of SafeArt and its wonderful programs encourage and allow people of all ages and from all walks of life who have been traumatized, paraphrasing Ernest Hemingway, to become **stronger at the broken places**."

Wynona Ward, Esq.
Director and Founder of Have Justice – Will Travel, Inc.

On Our Way...

An Anthology of *SafeArt* Writing 2000-2010

Edited by Tracy Penfield and Josey Hastings

4869 Main Street
P.O. Box 2200
Manchester Center, VT 05255

On Our Way...An Anthology of *SafeArt* Writing 2000-2010
©2010 SafeArt
Cover Photo: Nathalie Trottier
Blockprints: Tracy Penfield
Graphic Design: Heidi Allen Goodrich
All rights reserved
ISBN Number: 978-1-60571-078-5
Library of Congress Number: 2010911948

Building Community, One Book at a Time
This book was printed by the Northshire Bookstore, a family-owned, independent bookstore in Manchester Ctr., Vermont, since 1976. We are committed to excellence in bookselling. The Northshire Bookstore's mission is to serve as a resource for information, ideas, and entertainment while honoring the needs of customers, staff, and community.

Our Mission

SafeArt engages the transformative power of the arts in the prevention and healing of abuse and other traumas, through original performances, group and individual sessions, creative workshops and leader training, all designed to educate, to inspire and to heal people and their communities.

Contact Information:
SafeArt
PO Box 251 • Chelsea, VT 05038 • (802)685-3138
info@safeart.org • www.safeart.org

Contents

FOREWORD 7

PREFACE 10

COMING TO 12

RESCUE MISSION 16

REAWAKENED 19

IN MY TOWN 21

THE MOON 24

GO AWAY 26

BODY TAKEN 28

PULL AWAY 29

TRAPPED 31

HELP..32

DON'T HATE MYSELF ANYMORE 34

CHILD ABUSE 36

MY FIELD 37

DANCING ON MY FATHER'S GRAVE 40

IN CELEBRATION 41

DEAR DIARY 44

THE NIGHTMARE THAT ENDS WITH A DREAM.....................45

MY SILENCE 46

HEY BABY 48

MMMM MOTHER BEAR 50

DEAR MOM..52

FLASHBACKS	53
DEAR EX-LOVER	55
THE SAME WAY THE SKY CONTINUES TO BE	56
COMMUNION DANCE	59
ABUSED	60
THINGS I WISH I COULD SAY TO YOU	62
WATERFALL	65
SHE WATCHED	66
SPILT MILK	67
STRENGTH AND WORTH	69
DENIAL	70
FOR LIBERTY	72
STILLPOINT	75
SET HER FREE	77
ALL THE RIGHT THINGS	78
DIDN'T SEE IT COMING	80
TAKE FLIGHT	81
WORTH IT?	82
STURDY AND STRONG	84
CUTTING HER OUT	86
INVISIBLE SCARS	88
JUST BENEATH THE SKIN	90
EMACIATED BEAUTY	91
SKELETONS	92
THESE SHAKY HANDS	95

MY STORY	97
SUICIDE	99
MOTHER AND DAUGHTER	100
COMPLETE THE 360	103
WE ARE LIGHT	104
CONFRONTING YOU	106
GRAB YOUR LIFE AND RUN	107
FULL OF LOVE	108
WERE YOU THINKING ABOUT ME?	109
IT'S GOING TO BE COLD THIS WINTER (SO THEY SAY)	111
WATCH	112
EMPTINESS	115
FOREVER TIME	117
WHERE IT ALL ENDS	118
I CAN GET A GRIP	119
AS ONE MOMENT PASSES	121
ALCOHOLIC	124
THE MAN BEHIND THE BOTTLE	125
SMOKE RINGS	126
THE SECRET	127
BACK ROOMS	128
ON THE SHOULDERS OF MANY	130
WARM ME, WARM ME	132
ACKNOWLEDGEMENTS	135

Foreword

For the past 40 years I have worked as a therapist, in a variety of settings, with people of all ages seeking help for mental health and/or substance abuse issues. From my very first 'clients' to this day, I have always been struck by the prevalence of, and the inattention to, their histories of trauma.

We have thousands of studies and statistics documenting the widespread occurrence of abuse and other traumas. Most studies depend on self-report, but many who suffer do not see the connection between what has happened in the past and their current problems. Many don't understand that what they endured was in fact traumatic, and most never report what they often call "the worst stuff" – even when asked. As this age-old issue has become more public in the last few years, we are, finally, beginning to ask the questions. But when they do say, "Yes, I was abused" what are we offering people for healing?

Unfortunately, the mainstream treatment system has a tendency to ask, "What is wrong with you?" rather than "What has happened in your life?" In addition, there is a "let's move on" message that discourages people from talking about their past. And finally, there is the rampant use of psychoactive drugs to medicate our symptoms away. So we try to 'fix' eating disorders, bullying, domestic violence, sexual violence, alcohol/drug abuse, and many presumed symptoms of mental illness - anxiety, personality disorders, and depression to name the most common. Yet what is typically driving these problems are the fears, beliefs, behaviors, emotions, and unhealthy relationships, plus the ensuing addictions, that evolved to cope with unspoken, unresolved trauma.

In looking primarily at the presenting problems, to the exclusion of hearing the story, helpers are often trying to change what are actually reasonable adaptations to certain life experiences. Most of us do not give these up easily. Pain demands a remedy, and when neither the 'helpers' nor the 'clients' are aware of or can deal with the source of the pain, survivors will stick with whatever seems to help ease, ignore, deflect, or bury it.

Why do they so often not tell us what happened? Why are we loathe to ask? Are we afraid to speak about such matters? Perhaps we are all afraid to hear it out loud, because it is acutely uncomfortable? These are just some of the questions we need to ponder.

Having had the privilege of looking at many expressions of destructive life experiences (in poetry, journal entries, drawings, etc), it is not hard – but often shocking – to see what is being 'said.' I am heartened by the recent growth of Expressive Therapies as a recognized, credible approach to human healing. Why is this non-verbal, self-expression so critical? It is indeed a paradox, but through authentic, from-the-heart-and-guts "telling," shame is diminished enough to begin building, or re-claiming, a valued self.

In my experience, those who were encouraged to get their stories and feelings "out" made the fullest recoveries. Many credit their recovery with being encouraged to look at their past as a way to understand their present. When the past is fully understood, it no longer dictates our choices and beliefs. We can begin to take healthier charge of our lives.

SafeArt is a rare program dedicated to this principle and to the equally important element of sharing with other survivors that is so critical to letting go of pain. Whether in a group, on stage, through visual art, music, dance or writing, when our stories are acknowledged as truth and met without judgment, pathologizing, or avoidance, we are finally on our way. The content of this Anthology by *SafeArt* participants, who wanted their work published, gives us a glimpse into both the impact of trauma and the new-found courage and pride that come during the journey toward recovery.

I hope we all listen closely.

MaryJean McKelvy, MA, LCPC
Psychotherapist
Montpelier, Vermont
SafeArt Board Member

Preface

Abuse is pervasive in our time, as it has been in every time, yet humans possess a unique capacity for imagination, which can help us transcend traumatic experiences. Through artistic creativity, long-held emotional and physical responses to trauma can be accessed, expressed, and released.

SafeArt's programming creates a safe environment for this expression, in middle schools, high schools, colleges, in women's groups, retreats, and other venues. This body of work was selected from *SafeArt's* archives of pieces written during our first decade. They were chosen for the breadth of their content, and the authenticity of their forms. In *SafeArt* we have a saying, "Content rules!" We know that these works are not polished to a slick finish, and we have purposefully presented them in the form in which they were conceived, to allow the voice of the author to be heard, and felt.

Sharing the experience of abuse brings survivors together and embraces those who are isolated in their trauma. Publishing these pieces extends this sharing and educates those for whom abuse is something that happens to 'other' people, highlighting specific patterns of abusive behavior and traumatized responses.

Recently, we saw a man in his thirties, with his wife and two young sons. They are a beautiful family, loving, hard working and responsible. This man was among the first performers in *SafeArt's* early days. We first met 8 years ago, when he was referred to us by our local domestic violence agency. It was clear that he needed to heal. His mother had been murdered by her boyfriend, and this murderer was soon to be released from jail, on 'good behavior.' It was almost too much to bear, but bear it he did, and with encouragement, wrote his story. As he shared it with teens and adults in *SafeArt* audiences, his voice cracked, but he made it through, every time. And each time, he became calmer, stronger, more whole. To see him now, another 8 years later, with his family, is to witness the power of creative expression, and of love. He had wanted to kill his mother's murderer, but he chose another path, creative rather than destructive.

SafeArt reaches out to all people: victims, bystanders and perpetrators. We provide tools to prevent, halt, and heal traumatic abuse. Perpetrators tend to be unimaginative in their patterns of behavior, and if one is aware of these patterns, it is remarkably easy to detect an abusive situation. It is far more difficult to intervene, requiring courage, patience, and perseverance. However, everyone has the ability to be proactive and *SafeArt* offers safe, effective methods for making this choice. While never easy, being proactive is always an act of heroism.

Please take care of yourself when reading *"On Our Way…"*, as it could be overwhelming in its honest portrayals of abuse and trauma. There are also many words of hope and healing, as well as images upon which to rest one's thoughts.

Please let us know your response to this collection and visit our website, www.safeart.org. The youth and adult participants in *SafeArt*, whose pieces appear in this collection, all gave *SafeArt* permission to publish their work. We do so anonymously, except for the first and final pieces, which are two of *SafeArt's* 'signature' pieces, created by me in *SafeArt's* earliest days.

Thank you for joining us on our way to a more creatively expressive and compassionate society.

Tracy Penfield
SafeArt Founding Director
Summer 2010

Coming To

She went unconscious at the age of fourteen. She fell in love. From the very first date he manipulated her emotions, her beliefs, her behavior. He was also completely dependent upon her. She loved the simple certainty of it all. They would be together for life.

When she was seventeen, she came to -- enough to realize that he was an incorrigible ladies' man. She wanted to believe his promises of fidelity, but was briefly awake enough to attempt an escape. He followed her all the way across the country and hounded her until she conceded to return. When she was nineteen, he convinced her to marry him, and again she blacked out.

She could not, however, overlook the fact that she was happiest when he traveled for his work, a week, or two, or a month. She felt relaxed, industrious, at peace. What was wrong with her that she felt this way?

When he was home, the fighting intensified, the taunting, derisive, angry words hurled at her like stones, hitting with deep concussion. Objects began to fly: coffee mugs, books, tools, a chain saw. They did not hit her body, but their impact was profound. Her mind was in confusion. This was not the sort of behavior she expected from a civilized man. He was the son of a renowned scientist, working on his doctorate himself, while she worked to support them.

When she was twenty-one, she found herself pausing at the doorknob when she came home from work, wondering what type of weather she might encounter inside—a steady rain? A barrage of hail? A violent thunderstorm? He would reduce her to a rubble of emotion, then gather her up in his arms, saying how sorry he was, that he loved her more than anything in the world and that he would take care of her for life.

Doing battle aroused his lust, so the storms were followed by so-called love-making. She was numb. How could love and hate be so entwined?

He told her he did not like her constant singing.   She stopped.

And then there was the drinking and getting high that had been part of their relationship since the start. She actually preferred it when he was stoned—it made him dopey, dumb—not the sort of person she would choose to hang out with, but preferable to the mean, snarling man he became when drunk.

He dictated what clothes she should wear. His tastes ran to high cut skirts and low-cut blouses. Oh, he liked to see other men look her up and down, but flew into a jealous rage should she have a friendly chat with another man.

When she was twenty-six, she began to fantasize that he would die. She wished for his death by accident, any plausible accident she could think of. She did not consider murder, and although she contemplated suicide, it was not in her nature to carry out. It was difficult for others to see the desperate trouble she was in. She had no broken bones, no black eyes or purple bruises. Her wounds were internal, and she hid them well, yet wondered if she might cry herself to death.

One night, he destroyed a necklace made for her by a woman friend. He was in such a rage that she indeed feared for her life and ran to the neighbors' porch, leaned against their front door, heart pounding, yet did not awaken them. The next morning she asked this neighbor what he saw in her marriage. He quietly and gravely replied, "It is not a pretty sight."

In that instant, her mind began to clear. She came to, oh, so slowly. She knew that if they stayed together, she would die. Within a month she left.

He entreated her for many more months to return to him. She did not. His parting words to her were that she would henceforth be dead to him.

And so it was, at the age of thirty, I was reborn. I learned to crawl, then walk again. In time, I could run and even dance. Finally, I began again to sing.

*— Coming To **is the personal story of SafeArt Founder and Director Tracy Penfield. It is a performance piece with singing and dance.***

Rescue Mission

I.
there's a place
beneath the surface where
no woman should ever have to go
yet when i am taken there i
find flocks of us who've been
held down-pushed down-forced down
now i stand
the voice-line to our futures

my man
he said he was my man
said those three damn words yet i
swear it sounded more like a demand of
you love i
while intoxicated by my own dream
of truth in those words
i got sight of my freedom one day
saw it choking and strangling
in between his strong hands
holding no desire to respect
only to leave deep, dark blue-purple-green marks
upon my swelling determination to fly
i said baby if you loved me you wouldn't
hold me down-pin me down-push me down
i emerged from the vision of my freedom gasping for air
with only one request
set me free
let me free
get free

II.
these words meant nothing
nothing as you returned
over and over again to
hold me down
i'll fight you for it you said
fight me
fight me 'cause
right now my spirit's growin'
faster than your muscles ever could
think you're making marks on me
but my body's only these raging muscles
puncturing claws
the truth is my spirit's like sand
between your fingers
and the harder you squeeze the more
the blood that's bein' drawn is blood
from your nails diggin'
into your own hands
you hold my body down here
but i ain't anywhere near you anymore

III.
i thought it'd be a lonely place
a never-ending twisting spinning place
but i find i got company
while i'm a raging tigress to get free
from the filth of you on top of me
i find i'm communin' with girls
women and goddesses who know this territory
like they know the scent of pain swirling forth
from places where the only light
is the one we craft together
they give me strength

where i thought i only stood to lose
body beaten
i rise back up
stronger than when i went down
don't fuck with me
you think you've won but
my body now
fiercer than your body ever will be
i got lifetimes of animal souls
rushing back to me tellin'me
i'll never have to battle anyone or anything
alone
i'll fight you with their power
and
in the end
you'll be the one
to
go down

— 19 year-old woman

Reawakened

Remember, it's not your fault!
That you were raped
That I yelled and screamed
    Frenzied with frustration
That I lay there and took it
Because that's how I survived.

Then, I burst forth from the pumpkin shell
On wings like rainbows
High high into the sky
Spiraling like a runaway kite
No restraint
    No strings attached
        Untethered
Turning and turning and turning
Diving and soaring
With the wind against my face
Warmth of the sun
I land with assurance and confidence.
My pumpkin seeds take root
    Round and whole.
I soak up sun in safety
Swelling
Bathed in its warmth
My insides pressing me outward
And many children's voices
    Are reawakened
To sing and dance
    And tell
The story of their life.
It is time for harvest,

We are ripe
With hope!
Ready to move forward
We will carve our own stories
In the walking sticks
That support us.
When you are feeling down
I will loan you my walking stick.
Share my strength,
Plant pumpkin seeds of hope
In your garden
Your body alive
    With the greenness of spring.

And when it is dark
Our Love will
Illuminate the night,
Smoothing the edges of our fear,
Guiding our way.

— collaborative poem by adult women

In My Town

In my town, nothing is a secret.
A few thousand people,
a gas station, a creemee stand.
Everyone knows everyone and everything.
Rumors spread like fire, engulfing the entire village.
Non-facts about the people you know and see everyday.
Everything is taken with a grain of salt,
with a grain of deceit.
Like one man…

He owns the quaint general store.
Replacement mailboxes, milk, videos, beer.
His family is well-known.
Basketball stars, geniuses. Nice people. Popular kids.
His wife is clumsy. Bruises and lacerations.
The kids laugh, tell stories about her stumbling and tripping.
NO peripheral vision, they say.
When the topic comes up, the couple smiles at each other.
He strokes her hair, chuckles at her lack of balance.

They collect refugees, of a sort.
Vagabond kids whose parents were born and will
die in this town.
The kids of alcoholics, the ones that act out,
have bad home lives.
Always boys, always somehow internally scarred.
The general store man gives them jobs, a meal most nights.
Rumors about his past have gone around.
Some with conviction, some without.
Past jail time on rape, sexual assault charges.
Sexual assault on a little boy.

They might have been true, but probably not.
As teenagers, he gives us a place to party safely.
A wholesome, very Christian family,
using their rural land to let underage parties go unnoticed.
He provides the alcohol. We don't wonder why.
His young daughter dates grown men.
His middle son is an alcoholic, so young, worships him.
His oldest son, addicted to Jesus, defending his family,
but avoiding the topic of the rumors.

And then it was fact.
Suddenly, the charges against him sprang from the woodwork.
Boys he once cherished as his own,
Telling authorities how he molested them.
These vile truths wound through the town, through our lives,
like smoke.
A snake tightening its muscles so slowly
that we barely noticed until we couldn't breathe anymore.

My neighbor.
A man I've chatted with, drunk.
A man who hugged me on Halloween,
noticed my carefully calculated costume.
A man whose children I have spent time with,
eating pizza and watching sunsets.

And now
Boys I know
Boys I thought I knew…
He touched them. Hurt them. Raped them.
They won't ever be the same.
People glance, with pity, at those boys.
This man.
I traipsed around his store as a child,

There with dad to buy odds and ends.
This man
Whose pond I swam in,
Whose son I drank with,
Whose daughter I played sports with.

This man
Is a pedophile.
This man violates,
Controls,
Harms those who were already too weak
to deal with an untrustworthy adult.

In my town, everyone's lives are connected to everyone else's.
In my town, a man is going to prison
for his second charge of forcing young boys to appease his needs.
My town will never be the same.

He touched me
He raised me
He raped me
He loved me

— 16 year-old girl

The Moon

slowly you become the moon to me
watching over me at night
over everything i do
you watch over my dreams
you breathe upon my eyelids

the wine from your veins
makes my eyesight a little blurry
and i can't quite see you anymore
and i can't quite see the purple marks
the blue marks the red marks -
they look like love

slowly you become the moon to me
the waxing moon - growing larger
until you fill my whole night sky

— 16 year-old girl

Go Away

Go away, I tell you, go.
Don't touch me, go.
Go far away.
Where I can't see you.
I don't want to see you.
You hurt me.
My dreams are infected by you.
I just wish you would get away.
You don't listen to me.
When I cry I am hurt.
You take me out of my house
Into the woods and hurt me.
You say don't tell.
So I don't.
And I don't know what to do.
It keeps happening.
And I don't know how to tell.
Will it get worse if I tell?
I don't know
If my parents would think I was a liar.
What do I do?
My body says yes, tell.
But he says no, this is a little thing.
Ssssshhh, he says.
What do I do?
I am all mixed up.
Yes.
No.
It is all running around in my head.
What should I do?
Every day this happens.

Why to little young me?
That is it, I am little.
Little people don't tell.
I am pretty.
I keep saying
Go away.
That is what keeps coming out of my mouth.
But finally after getting hurt for a week,
I tell.
My parents did believe me.
And he never came back, never!

— 15 year-old girl

Body Taken

No. No.
I said no.
I screamed it.

Could you not hear me? You couldn't.
Body taken. Voice muted. Was I not human? Inhuman.

Demanding, Forcing.
Prizes undeserved.
You didn't deserve me.

Flashing lights.
They caught you running.
My screams delivered me – heard by human ears capable of mercy.
They can punish you like I can't.

While you sit in your prison, I sit in mine – my own body.
Now alien.

violent lust. broken trust. in the world.

was it worth it to you. was it worth it to you. was it worth it to you.

— 18 year-old woman

Pull Away

At the age of four, she didn't know what he was doing.
She didn't know it was bad.
It happened when her mom left to go to the store or to visit her grandmother.
Years have gone by.
Now she is fourteen.
This mostly happens when he is drunk.

The girl's mom has been gone for a few days to go help her grandmother. He has bought the girl cigarettes and alcohol so he can get what he wants. He comes home from a long day at work. She walks through the door with a couple of friends. He asks them to leave 'cause they need to talk about something. He has been drinking. She can smell it on his breath. She knows what is going to happen. She doesn't know how to say no. She's tried before, but he threatened her. She doesn't have a way to escape the pain.

She hears her friends walking down the street. They are right by the window. Lacy, Louise, and Shauna come and ring the doorbell. She is crying when she goes to the door. Louise knows something has happened. She has her suspicions about things. The girl is told to come back by 12, no later. She says okay, love you Dad.

He sits and waits. It's about 11:30 now and he's too drunk and on some pills. He falls asleep. She tries to be as quiet as possible, but the door creaks and wakes him up. By then she's in a dark corner hoping and praying he falls back to sleep. He does. She goes upstairs and falls asleep. Shortly after, she's awakened by very cold hands. She cries and tries to pull away.

The family tells her that they were evicted. They weren't.
She's staying at a friend's house. She gets a phone call from her older sister asking if she wants to live with Aunt Donna. She says yes. Her older sister called her because she couldn't deal with all the pain that she saw the girl was going through.
He's now in jail 5 to 15 years. That 14-year old girl was me.
I'm now 16, living the normal life that *she* always wanted. I'm in the healing process.

— 16 year-old girl

Trapped

He's home
I'm alone
I fear
What is near
He throws me on the ground
He's all around
My clothes get ripped
As I am stripped
He touches me
He rides me
He says if I tell anyone
He'll get a gun
He'll put it to my head
And that will be the end

— 14 year-old girl

Help

Help me
> I'm trapped
> Forever
> In a society
> Full of indifference
> And uncontrasting people

Help us
You've captured
Our individuality
We are inferior
Under your power

> Help them
> See their beauty
> Their interior self
> Stop the judgment

Help yourself
You're blind
To your domination
Stop the judgment

— 13 year-old boy

Don't Hate Myself Anymore

From age eight
To age twelve
She dreaded Sundays
Every single Sunday
She'd go downstairs with him
She didn't want to
She didn't have a choice
She was forced down
She was abused
She hated it
She hated him
She wanted to throw him off
She wanted to tell
She was angry
She was scared
She felt sick
She felt dirty
She would make excuses
Not to go down
Down to her personal hell
How could he do this?
Her own cousin
How?
She hated it
She hated him
She wanted to throw him off
She wanted to tell
She was angry
She was scared
She felt sick
She felt dirty

Downstairs in the basement
Dark and cold
He would belittle her
So many times
She said no

Finally I told
In eighth grade I told
I told my counselor
I told my friends
I got help
I still hate him
But I don't hate myself
Anymore

— 15 year-old girl

Child Abuse

There is a sense of loneliness,
shame, guilt, and fear,
but above all it is the sense
of filthiness,
the repulsiveness,
towards your own self.

The experience makes you feel like a pile of manure,
that you've rolled in it
and can never wash it off.
You've been dragged through the mud,
over and over again.
It's on your skin,
in your mouth, in your body.

You can never be rid of it.

— 15 year-old girl

My Field
A performance piece

Woman ~ (walking across stage, stops to look at hand.)

I glanced at my right thumbnail and thought about this morning when I broke it, lugging in firewood. Bending it back over sure hurt, but at least it didn't break down into the quick; that is even more painful.

Inner Voice ~ Yeah, but it still doesn't hurt as much as having your wrists tied together.

Woman ~ Yes, you're right…hey, wait a minute! Who are you? What do you mean, having your wrists tied together?

Inner Voice ~ You know, like Momma used to do when we were bad.

Woman ~ No! I don't know what you mean! (under breath) This is crazy!

Inner Voice ~ Momma used to tie our hands and not let us go pee, and then be mean when we wet our pants.

Woman ~ I don't know what to say…

Both voices unison ~ I have to go to the bathroom, please Momma, please, please let me go now.

Woman ~ Suddenly it was like I was transported back in time…(sits down, crosses wrists)
I am sitting in my Daddy's chair. But Daddy isn't there, only

Momma and I are there and she is washing dishes. I look down at my hands. They are tied about the wrists with dirty white shoelaces. The lacings are tight and my hands and fingers are turning red and blue and the ends are going to sleep. I have on a faded t-shirt that is ripped at the neck and sleeve, but the blue corduroy pants look bright and new. I look up at my Momma~

Please, Momma, please, I need to go pee.

Mother's Voice ~ Piss, piss, piss, that's all I ever hear! All I ever do around here is clean up after everybody. Look at this filthy place. Piss, piss, piss, that's all I ever smell!

Woman ~ But Momma, please I need to go now, I promise I will be good, I won't be bad anymore. Please, Momma, I don't want to wet my new pants.

Mother's Voice ~ New Pants, new pants. Think you're pretty smart getting new pants, don't you, just cause you're daddy's favorite. Well, just wait until he comes home tonight and smells those new pants!

Woman ~ (slowly uncrosses wrists and stands up to walk across stage, speaking to audience) I do not recall ever feeling so helpless and alone. Besides, being Daddy's favorite wasn't exactly fun. He raped me for the first time when I was three. From the time I was four until I was twelve, I had a secret place called 'My Field'. In My Field I was safe and no one could get me. No one could tell me I was bad. It was always summer in My Field and the sun warmed me through and through. There were only nice sounds in this safe haven of mine.

The first time I found My Field, my body was hanging in the

cold, dark cellar in the old house where I grew up. (stops and lifts left shoulder, standing on tiptoe)

I am hanging by the back of my shirt, and by a blue scarf around my neck with a knot in the end, looped around a nail. If I try to get down, I can't breathe very well. There is a crack of light coming from under the pantry door. I can see my father's rubber boots hanging on a nail, just like me. I'm glad I'm not hanging alone...

I wish so much I hadn't been bad—although I'm not sure what I've done. But I must be bad because my mother said so, and then she got mad and hung me here.

I can hear my baby sister screaming in the kitchen and I want to help her. I want to tell my mother to hurt me, not to hurt her. I don't want my mother to tie her up and do the things to her that she always does to me. Then the cellar door opens and my mother hangs my sister next to me. It hurts to talk so I just smile at her and reach out and touch her arm.

I was four years old when my mother tied me up and stuffed me in a bureau drawer. I went to My Field. When I was six, my grandmother locked me in a dark closet for telling 'lies' about what my mother did to me. When I was nine, my grandfather raped me. The pain was too much to bear. I went to My Field.

The mind is a miraculous thing. In My Field I was safe. There was no physical pain. It was always warm. In My Field, I could be me, and I was a good girl. In My Field, I was not helpless and I could feel loved.

— created from narratives of a 50 yr. old woman

Dancing on My Father's Grave

dancing on my father's grave
to the tune of my spirit
my body twisting and twirling
my arms swinging my hands like butterfly wings
gliding through my past
dancing
floating to the rhythms of my friends
all in the ether of release

dancing on my father's grave
not in anger for the years of neglect or pain
but spinning in the narrow shaft
of the light of love
that somehow found its way

dancing on my father's grave.

— adult man, written for a woman friend

In Celebration

There was the honey and cheese that fed my mother as I grew within her
and the people, stoic and strong, who cared for her as a child,
and the long line of ancestors that stretches back to France
and other countries that existed before France,
a wandering line that wends so far back into history
that it gets lost amid the fins and flippers, green muck
and endless seas,
tossing and turning in the dark.

And then there was me,
twirling in my own dark sea, my flippers turning into hands
to form these words on paper, to love and to work,
to bring food to my mouth, to touch the infinite grains of sand,
the sliminess of seaweed, the warmth of a lover's skin.

There is every life ever given to me,
to sustain my life, whispering yes, continue on, grow and grow –
sheep and goats, pigs, cows, chickens, even a deer or
two and a moose,
fish and octopus, mollusks, carrots and beets,
leaves of so many shapes and textures,
apples and berries, mangos and avocados.

There is the love that greets me every morning,
in the sun itself and in the knowledge of other human beings
concerned with my health and survival, my joy and learning.
There is the family that has given me a home
in the geography of this world and the territory of the heart.

There are the precious resources that have sent me whizzing
through the sky to find a soul that could touch mine in
all its rawness
and across fields and mountains, broken in two by our
ribbons of transit,
on errands of intense depth and of frivolity.

There is the beauty offered up each day, in a blue jay's wing,
in a lamb's quiet gaze, in the lacy skirts of mushrooms,
beauty gifted to us in every moment, if we care to notice.

And there is the protection and guidance, so long unperceived,
that have brought me to this day, that have shepherded me
through the trees of dark depressions,
that have informed my heart,
that have shown me passion and the beauty of my soul.

May these small words speak my gratitude,
may they spread it like seeds to the sun, the wind,
the earth, and waters,
may it be carried to each corner of existence,
to the intimate interior of every cell,
that all may receive back the smallest shard of what I
have been given.

— 29 year-old woman

Dear Diary

Dear Diary,

Sometimes I find myself outside just to catch a breath of fresh air. I feel the blades of grass closing in around my bare feet. I look up into the night sky and I see a shooting star. And I think to myself, "I want to be that shooting star. I want to get away from here and go as far and as fast as I can."

I look at the other houses. They look warm and comforting. Our house looks dark and cold. It is always this way after a fight. He gets drunk and yells and throws things. I try my hardest not to get him more upset. The house is hot with anger and rage. Then he storms out and the house becomes cold, empty, and stale.

He is gone right now. I could leave. It is what my friends would want me to do. But I'm not brave enough, strong enough. I know he will find me. I want to get out, but I don't know how.

Dear Diary,

I feel so free now. Although I am confined to a hospital bed, beaten and bruised, I feel an incredible sense of freedom, as if I were made of a thousand shooting stars. He is gone now. He will not find me. I look forward to a life without the emptiness and anger. I will be braver. I will be stronger. My life will be filled with laughter, warm houses, soft grass, fresh air, night skies, and, of course, shooting stars.

— 16 year-old girl

The Nightmare That Ends with a Dream

They kiss me goodnight.
They're going out dancing,
But what they don't know
Is what he'll do after they leave.
I hate it when they go.
I get into trouble and misbehave,
Hoping they'll ground me, that they'll stay,
But it's a special day,
Their anniversary,
And we both know
They'll be gone for awhile.
I lie in the dark listening,
Waiting to hear the car drive away,
Waiting for my nightmare to begin,
For the footsteps to get closer.
The steps of the devil.
The door opens, he comes in,
And it all starts.
I drift away.
I fly to a place where I am free,
Free of him, and the hell he brings upon me.
I am happy again. I am relieved.
Magic all around me. Peaceful, relaxing.
I am in heaven,
in a soft dream full of magic and wonder, love and care.
I float there and pray that there I will stay forever,
Never cry myself asleep again,
And never be touched by that snake again.

— 15 year-old girl

My Silence

He is my friend
I don't want to be involved
I don't know him good enough
I am not his family

He is so nice to me
To everybody

I don't know for sure
I don't know if it is happening

I am not sure
Not sure
Not sure that he beats her up
Leaves bruises on her
Abuses her
Sexual
Physical
Intimidates her   threatens her   humiliates her
Rapes her
I am not sure
He is my friend
I don't want to lose him

He seems so nice
I don't believe it
I am just a friend
I am afraid

I can't interfere
It is his privacy

I saw the news today
I saw my friend
He killed her
Beat her to death   raped her
My friend

I might have said something
But it was his privacy

Now I am sure
I am sure it was her mind
Her body
My silence

— 17 year-old boy

Hey Baby

I can be your Victorian ballerina
Graceful peace to ease your furrowed brow
Your day has been long

Hey baby

I will dance on my toes
I will dance on eggshells
I will dance around in circles for you

Hey baby

You will offer me bouquets of roses
And turquoise bracelets daily
Your drunken lips kissing mine

Hey baby

Our house will be built on cement
Secure, like your "love" and "affection"
And you will come home from the office, a long day's work

Hey baby

The door will slam behind your entrance
Dinner will have been ready for over an hour
Your lips will grimace with displeasure

Hey baby

My Sunday morning will be spent cleaning
The glass and china littering the floor
The bathroom a mess from the cut lip you gave me

Hey baby

You will croon me to sleep at the end of the day
Your hands rubbing my feet
You will pamper me in your own affectionate way

Hey baby

You ask for forgiveness
Your sad brown eyes wanting me
Forcing me to maintain eye contact

— 16 year-old girl

Mmmm Mother Bear

Mmmm Mother Bear
Feasting, feasting, feasting
Instinctively feasting

You who know no shame
Your wildness sublime
Walking this Earth with your wisdom
Be my companion on this journey

Teach me about ferocity
And to dance in the moonlight
And to go to sleep at night
With cubs in your arms

Embrace me as well
With your intuitive love

> *— collaborative poem by adult women in a SafeArt retreat*

Dear Mom

Dear Mom,

I don't know if I ever told you how much I loved you, Mom. It probably wouldn't have made a difference, anyway. I know you felt trapped, but why didn't you leave and take us with you? You left me alone with him, Mom. I feel so helpless. I need your guidance. I need to know what to do. But you didn't know what to do either, did you? How can he have so much control? I can't leave, Mom. He'll go after the others. I'm too young to be in charge. I don't know what to do. I've been protecting the kids, Mom. Aren't you proud of me? I learned from you. You never let him touch us. And I'll never let him touch them. I'm going to be strong, Mom. I'm going to live. I'm not going to leave them all alone, Mom. Not like you did.

'Laurel'

— 16 year-old girl

Flashbacks

I looked up, but I couldn't bear to see
The sight that was in front of me.
I ran away with all my speed,
But you caught up and took the lead.
I could not run away from you.
If only you knew the things you do.
This is the only way I can tell you:

The wedding night you hid your drink.
    Flashback!
Mom is pouring Dad's beer into the sink.

The day I caught you smoking pot.
    Flashback!
There are bags of grass in Daddy's car. Mom says he was caught.

Last night you said you'd drink in the car.
    Flashback!
Six years old, Daddy takes me to a bar.

Today you got mad and pushed your brother down.
    Flashback!
I don't know why Daddy's mad enough to throw me to the ground.

Today I tried to get away, but you reached out and gripped my arm.
    Flashback!
His hands left marks and bruises. He told Mom he meant no harm.

My friends tell me to leave you. They say you are no good.
    Flashback!
I begged my Mom to get rid of Dad. She said she never could.

They say if your Daddy hurts your Mom, your husband will hurt you, too.
I promised myself it wouldn't happen to me, so what do I say about you?

— 15 year-old girl

Dear Ex-Lover

Dear Ex-Lover,

I know we haven't spoken for years. You've probably moved on, met another woman, or many other women, or even had children. Maybe your career is going well, you're making money. Maybe you've bought a house or a new car.

I've also moved on, but it took me awhile. You see, when we broke up, I felt I had no reason to live. I asked myself, "How could I possibly exist on my own? Without you?"
Because like you told me so many times, in so many different ways, I didn't matter.

To you, I was nothing more than a mouse or an insect. A waste of air. Nothing I could do could make me better in your eyes. I deserved it, you said, the pain you inflicted upon me. If only I were smarter, prettier, stronger, richer, then maybe I would be your equal. Then, maybe, you would look at me with love in your eyes.

Anyway, I am writing to tell you something important, something about me. I figured it out after our relationship ended. It's why we never worked as a couple. It is why, I think, you felt you had to hurt me.

What I have to tell you is this: I am a wonderful human being. I'm independent. I'm self-sufficient. I'm smart, funny, beautiful, even. And I don't rely on any man to tell me this. And now that I know all of this about myself, I want to forgive you. You saw these things in me, even before I did. It scared you, threatened you. So you hurt me. I understand.

I would be scared of me, too.

— 18 year-old woman

The Same Way the Sky Continues to Be

So young once...
I hadn't seen you for a month
and I had been around the world and back,
seen so much and learned and changed...
but there you were.

On my doorstep,
baggy, black jeans and a Nirvana shirt on a 90 degree day,
brown hair fastened at the nape of your neck, a few
frizzy curls escaping,
black rubber band straining at the thickness of your strands.
Humid air hung like curtains of gray around us.
I pulled a curtain aside and stepped out,
on the cracked asphalt sidewalk and under the blank sky,
closer to you.

We walk, the looming threat of rain, the air pressure changing,
the air transforming from its stagnant stance,
gray curtains billowing out, filling up,
sails moving a pirate ship.

We walk, over the cracks,
not much passes over our throats and through our mouths.
I clutch the spiral notebook, blue with celestial angels
on the cover,
my journal, my thoughts, my poems, close to my chest.
Finally I unclench and I drop the book into one hand
and you grab my other hand.

We turn our faces up toward the empty sky,
which is suddenly filling with raindrops
appearing like magic in the sticky air,
cooling our bodies, calming our spirits
and suddenly I find my voice again and you find yours,
because so much has happened, has changed, has remained.

The shelter of a large maple,
with huge green bunches of hands atop its wooden body,
beckons to us and we find ourselves under it,
safe and only damp, not soaked after all.
A drop escapes through the outstretched fingers above us,
landing on an angel, reminding me
of all my thoughts of you, forever looting my love,
but I don't care because I have an endless supply,
the same way the sky continues to be,
the wind continues to blow,
the rain continues to fall,
I will always continue to love.

— 25 year-old woman, while in prison

Communion Dance

I do believe angels weaved right through us

In the gentle slowness
Of a beat with no rhythm
So fine and delicate, our hands were left holding grace

I do believe the Goddess was watching
And joined us as our spirits merged
Because I smiled and it came all the way up from my heart

And the wind enveloped that glimmer of joy

With a healing shawl of woven sky
With diamond threads that linger
Sewing us into ecstasy

I do believe angels weaved right through us

— collaborative poem by adult women in a SafeArt retreat

Abused

abuse is a tool used
when a fuse is disconnected
thoughts and feelings of being rejected
and not protected
but a hand is directed
straight connected to a child's smile
all while you live in denial
and let your anger
put your kid's life in danger
probably better off living with a stranger
but if you got that better understanding
and knew that those futures were our planning
for this planet
you wouldn't take them for granted
so you need to just can it
and find better ways
before you spend the rest of your days
locked up
should have thought about that before getting her knocked up
but don't mistake my intake for trying to relate
I'm just trying to create
that better understanding, demanding
that we educate, speak out, articulate
maybe we all should just unwind
for a little meditation
relaxation helps the prevention
need not mention that the suspension's
still to come
see there was this wife
who had a deadbeat husband for a life
'cause she stayed home and cooked and cleaned

while he went out and made the green
and every night he came home, blew off some steam
but you wouldn't hear her scream
'cause the abuse was done mentally
potentially making her crazy
but inside she was a sweet beautiful lady
somehow got mixed up with a guy who was shady
now he's saying he wants to start having a baby
but she told him not lately
'cause when the fighting got physical
she only wished she was invisible
living like that made her life so unlivable
'cause he'd given her a beating
thinking she was cheating
but she'd always be home sweeping
and now weeping
from watching the TV shatter
the glass was scattered
and she was left beaten and battered
alone in the comfort of her own home
thinking to herself this can't be good for my health
so she left with no trace on where she would be
packed up and said goodbye to those fucked up memories

— *18 year-old man, performed as 'spoken word'*

Things I wish I could say to you

Why? Why do you say that to me every time you see me?

Are you trying to hurt me? Do you think it's funny?
Do you think you're a better person than I am?

Do you believe that it's okay to be different?
What do you know about me anyway?
You think that I am gay. So what? Have you been taught that gay is wrong?

Do you really believe that the things you have been taught are all there is to know?
You're just one person living in this big world—you need to open your ignorant eyes.
The words you throw at me feed hate and pain and murder.
Many people have died because other people could not accept their differences.
We live in a country that aims to accept all people and gives them the freedoms to live. Do you value the freedom to be yourself?
To be different? Do you even realize it?

You may be uncomfortable with the fact that some people are different.
Does that give you the right to say what's right and wrong?

Are you expressing your opinion or do you have your own problems?
What kinds of insults have you suffered that you need to come here and insult me?
What kinds of insecurities do you have that you have to cut

me down to make yourself feel better?
I will never forget you. This is who you will always be to me.

Your words land upon my back like rocks. Some roll off, some leave bruises. Sometimes I take comfort in the fact that you don't really know what you are saying.
Sometimes that makes it even worse.

I am a person, like you. I am unique and different.

I have depth and character. The world is large and life grows in many ways.

I will not attack you for being different than I am.

— 26 year-old man

Waterfall

Bullies are a waterfall
Running with rage.
Their angry curves and currents
Shall soon fall
To keep them flowing.
They think bringing down
Others will help them to climb higher,
But each time they try
They just fall down lower.
Bullies are the helpless.
They are always falling,
For their anger blinds them.
They are the true victims.

— 12 year-old boy

She Watched

She stood by and watched
She always watched
She couldn't remember a time she didn't watch
She wanted to help, but she couldn't
She saw the person wearing down
More and more
She looked at the bullies
She wanted to move them, to stop them
She stepped out of the crowd of bystanders
As she came closer to the bullies she felt more feelings
She gently took the person's hand
She led her away from the bullies and the crowd
She knew now she would never again just stand
and watch

— 13 year-old girl

Spilt Milk

Windowless, and gasoline fumes -
    you had my pants,
    your hand pulsing, curled, coke-stained fingernails
        and a curious cocker spaniel the only witness.

You pushed
    my first kiss and I
broke like some fallen egg,
too much for even the Main Street bum.

Would Mrs. Lee
the unsuspecting dog-sitting employer
    come on time
    come on, hurry
mouth rubbed tired
pants sagging.
Expose me - a look into eyes cluttered with a lost eyelash.
    I guess they end at the brown.

You asked me if I was a lesbian.
        We could be friends.
My friend Ruth was held down in elementary school locker rooms,
12 year olds with razors cut her leg hair.
Ruth joined the wrestling team.

Had I said yes would you have not
had my
head stuck, and down on a welcome mat,
and buzzing next to the unplugged lawn mower?

Was it your dad,
left you?
    He loved money,
you said with the waves at our toes,
the sand in our eyes,
the familiar rock behind the splintering stairs.

I remember your green front door,
your mom,
a wide open silk blue bathrobe.

Just after the walk on the beach,
my hands push into the fumes of Mrs. Lee's garage
the last of the sand shaking from my toes.

— 16 year-old girl

Strength and Worth

They yell, they scream,
they come to you with a sword.
They swing, they stab,
they slice you through the heart.
You know it's over,
you're gone, you've lost,
but then you find in yourself
that someone, something must care.
This can't be the only thing.
You pull the sword from your heart,
healing as you go
and drop it to the floor.
You've done it, you've made it.
They came to you with a sword of words,
but you came to them with strength and worth.

— 16 year-old boy

Denial

She cries now, herself to sleep,
as you finish another bottle
and you down another drink.
Then you begin to yell
like you said you never would.
She is very strong
and you said you'd get help,
but that never happened.
Now you say you only wanted
to teach her a lesson.
That's what you told her, isn't it,
when you nearly pushed her down the stairs.
You just sat there then
while she stared, eyes bewildered,
lost in her trance,
until you broke
the silence
and said she made you do it.
With all her might she holds her anger back.
You hurt her every time you drink
and every morning you say the same thing.
"I never meant to hurt you."
"I never meant those mean things I said."
"I swear I'll never do it again."
But that's what you said last time.
The girl begins to wonder
will the madness ever end
and then begins to cry.
She soon wishes she could die.
So I now must draw the line.
I know what you do,

but only stay in denial,
for her love for you is strong.
This I know,
but you do not.
I tell you this
from the goodness of my heart.

— 17 year-old girl

For Liberty

You confuse me and you make me laugh.
You understand when I feel like I'm half
of a person. Sometimes it happens in here,
too much wasted time this year.

You make me remember that I still exist,
a shot of reality, better than tequila bliss!
Because you're not fake like all the rest,
you're not havin' that, you get things off your chest.
You stand up for your beliefs and for that I am proud
to call you a friend, one I don't want to do without.

Your name means freedom,
so ironic considering the doors
that are perpetually locked,
the light that doesn't warm our skin,
the smells that we have learned to miss:
perfume, cookies, cologne, incense.
The clothes, the make-up, all the material things
we indulged in, don't mean anything anymore,
because we can't leave these metal doors.

They try to trick us into believing we're not in jail,
pastel paint "brightening" up our spaces,
food that puts pounds on the hips and smiles on our faces,
a couple of bunks, they tell us it's like a dorm room,
but there's still wire on the windows
and locks everywhere you look.
Maybe you can escape in a book?
Your eyes tell it all, dark pools with a story,
if only you dive in deep.

Independent and pure, your smiles I will keep
so close to my heart, forever in my memory.

Trapped together in this place,
we've made the most of our space.
Our pain twists and coils through our stomachs,
but we ignore it for another day,
choosing instead to listen to the rain
that splatters on tin in our minds,
loud, but soothing.
Thoughts keep coming in, flooding us out, numb.

A loud beat plays in my head.
I think you hear it too, so we dance,
play their games, bide our time,
until we can run in the rain in our head,
the pigs checking our beds,
and our imprisonment ends.
A beautiful disaster,
that's what you are.
No matter where I am,
I will always look up and find your star.

— 25 year-old woman, while in prison

Stillpoint

The stillness, the stillness of the stillpoint
That place where you are neither here nor there
That place where neither past nor present exist
It is here in this space where you are caught in the dance
Caught in the dance between that which is known
And that which is unknown
Suspended in time

The stillness, the stillness of the stillpoint
Surrounded in the black of darkness
Where only the crystal white of the glimmering stars
Dares to show you the way
And it is only up to you
Whether you allow yourself to follow the way
The way of light

The stillness of the stillpoint
Caught in the pivot of the dance
Where all movement has stopped
Suspended in time at that crucial moment
In that place between who you are
And who you were meant to be
It is here and only here where you have the choice
Do you stay in the comfort of darkness
Or do you take the chance

And so, it is in the stillness, the stillness of the stillpoint
Where you make that choice
Where you take that tiny step
To embrace the dance
Where the tiniest of movements

Suddenly rotates you off the pivot
And head first you are tumbling down and down
Through the blackness and the glimmering light of the stars
Through the heat of the red molten lava
Through the bleak iciness of the past
And out into the light forever.

— 50 year-old woman

Set Her Free

The time has come to break the
Silence.
I finally have a voice.
As a child I would cry out,
But to everyone around me it was just noise.
Shattered and broken by rejection,
I locked it up inside myself,
Telling myself I had no choice.
Years went by and deeper I hid
That dirty little secret.
And so, transformed to a teenager,
I became a girl with no self-respect.
Then one day I heard a voice inside me say
"Let that little girl free!"
So I found a way to talk
About the pain inside of me
And how to heal the grief.
Believing in myself,
Now I have finally found the strength to set her
Free.

— 30 year-old woman

All the Right Things

he did all the right things
he did everything right
took care of her kids
held her close and tight
told her that he loved her unconditionally

then something went wrong
just about one year
and now every time I see her
silent screams I hear

and all the pain
and all the heartache
just won't fade
and I can't stop it
all the pain

a man called their home
he assumed the worst
and the impact of his fist
was not as bad as the impact of his words

— 17 year-old boy

Didn't See it Coming

You say that you love me,
I say your love hurts.
Sometimes you get physical,
even mentally you burn.
I don't understand you.
You say you're sorry and you'll stop.
You know I'm scared,
you really blew the top.
Sometimes when you hit me,
I wonder what you'll do next.
I just cannot leave you,
and our love cannot be fixed.
I didn't see it coming,
didn't think you were the type.
It was perfect in the beginning,
we didn't even fight,
but now it's every day
you put your hands on me.
You will soon find out
how it's gonna be.
I need to get away.
Soon I will fly.
Once I loved you dearly,
now I say goodbye.

— 15 year-old boy and girl collaboration

Take Flight

She smiles as her heart gets broken.
She laughs when he forgets she is there.
She hides in his shadow
as he looks at her with his terrifying glare.

She shuts her eyes as he shouts and screams.
She won't open them 'til morning.
She hides her bruised face in broken dreams.
For a more complete life, she is longing.

When he is gone for days on end
she can be herself so freely.
She lives in her secret world
and she doesn't have to hide her feelings.

In the hidden place of her mind,
she knows he has to go.
She feels a longing to leave him behind.
When she leaves, maybe then he'll know

How she really feels,
like she is about to break,
but now like a new person,
she begins to take flight.

— 17 year-old girl

Worth it?

Play the bass loud, make my whole body pound.
Make my heart fill with sound, so I don't have to think.

Tear my life apart 'cause it sucks right now.
I wanna heal my pain, but I don't know how.
I'm thinkin' of all these things you said were true.
Maybe I am nothing without you.

And I can hit the drums so hard that I can't feel my hands,
and I can scream so loud that I can't hear myself,
and I can cry so hard that I can't even breathe,
           but none of it's worth it,
'cause I can still see your face in my head,
all the horrible things that you said.
             Why can't I just be free?

Why do I dream of you?
      If I only knew…
           If I could figure out…

Why I feel like crap,
why I wanna cry
'til I'm oh so tired
I wanna sleep forever.
Forever is such a long time, forever.
Will I feel like this forever?
Did he change my life forever?
Am I broken now forever?

Forever, forever, please help me, forever.
I changed. I just wanna be back to myself.
And life seemed so hard for those few weeks.
I swore I would not make it through.
I needed to be alone for awhile,
but the truth is I didn't have to be.
My heart opened up as they came to me,
my friends surrounding me with love.
And sometimes life's tough, it just gets me down,
but as long as friends are here, I'll try darn hard to get up.

And when I hit the drums now, I wanna feel my hands,
and when I don't scream loud, I wanna hear kind words,
and I'm so glad when I cry that someone will hold me,
        'cause it makes it all worth it,
        they make my life worth it.

— 16 year-old girl, song lyrics

Sturdy and Strong

The tree is in the middle of nowhere,
but somewhere.

Nothing around to make a sound,
except for a small fluttering butterfly,
fluttering by before the storm has a chance to settle in.

The sky is getting grayer
where the warm breezes turn to violent gusts of wind,
but the tree stands sturdy and strong.

The tree is not in harm's way,
but in the middle of it at the same time.

The butterfly has gone now,
and the small, light raindrops slowly
start to accompany the tall, lonesome tree.

A small robin flies into the tree's bushy leaves,
and sits over a little nest
with three tiny blue eggs inside.

The storm passes and the sun comes out.

The tree is in the middle of nowhere,
but somewhere.

And nothing around to make a sound,
except for a small fluttering butterfly,
fluttering by just to say goodbye.

— 16 year-old girl

Cutting Her Out

The cuts I make are deep and clean.
I try to cut the hate out.
It's still there.
She's still there,
With the mean, hateful words she snarls at me.
Her words.
"Stupid
Insignificant
Unwanted
Who could ever love you?
Who would ever want someone like you?
Your friends don't care.
You're the naïve kid with extra money.
They don't care about you,
And why would they?
Look at you.
And if they ever knew
What you really are
They would see how
Pathetic
Stupid
Self-doubting
Suicidal
Insignificant you really are.
What a waste of a human being,
You nothing."
All of her words spinning around in the background of my life.
The cutting got worse,
but her words cut deeper than I could.
The cutting stopped,
But she didn't.

The louder she got, I thought others would hear.
The panic attacks started.
They got worse the louder she got.
There was no face I could put to her,
Only the voice coming from the darkness.
She seemed undefeatable.
I was tired, broken and beaten down,
Trapped.
I had never spoken of
Her
But one day I decided I was done.
I unmasked her,
Named her.
I took my power back.
I shattered her.

— 16 year-old girl

Invisible Scars

She wears long-sleeved shirts to hide the pain she
brings on herself.
The smile she wears has the same purpose.
"I'm worthless," she thinks to herself -
the first blade that cuts deep, but leaves invisible scars.

She knows she has a problem, but that only makes it worse.
The scars are reminders of what she has done, the past
she can't hide.
She tells everyone she is okay when she really wants to scream.

"I'm afraid of the truth," she tells herself.
"I don't want anyone else to get hurt."

She doesn't realize how much she is loved, how much
her friends care.
"Why won't you tell me what's happening?" he asks her over
and over again.

"I don't want to hurt you. I never know what emotion I'm
going to have!"

She hears him say he wants to help, but the little creature
in the back of her head,
the demon that's always there, silences her with fear.
"He doesn't really care," it says, screams.
She struggles, fights back.
"I don't need this anymore. Go away!" she screams in her
internal struggle.
"You're worthless," the demon whispers in her ear.

He's waiting for an answer.
He can see her fighting with herself.
"I'm here if you need me. Don't worry about hurting me."
She relaxes, but then puts on her fake smile, says "Thanks,"
and walks away.

Soon enough, her arms are full of scars,
little pink ribbons screaming every insecurity she has ever felt.
"This can't keep going forever," a small voice says in her head
as she picks herself up from the bathroom floor.

She has to tell him, believe that he will understand.

He can tell something is wrong. He sees right through her mask.

It's a relief for her knowing he can tell, but telling him the
truth is so hard.

She tries to tell him and bursts into tears, losing all control.

"I'm here," he says, wrapping his arms around her.
"I will always be here."

"I'm done doing this," she says…she shows him her arms.

— collaborative poem by 16 year-old girl and boy

Just Beneath the Skin

You look and see a happy girl
surrounded by friends and content with the world,
but the things you don't know,
that's where it begins,
because the memories that haunt her
lurk just beneath the skin.

The scars are nonexistent except inside
where no one can see them,
where she can hide.
Smiling and laughing, you'd think nothing awry
because she refuses to let herself cry.
She straightens her shoulders and sets her chin,
determined not to let it get to her again.
The words that cut her soul like knives -
seems as though they were in a different life,
but some things trigger memories of her past.
She's convinced that the trauma will not last.

So, next time she shies away from random things
or recoils from the harshness another voice brings,
just remember the things you don't know
is where it begins,
because the memories that haunt her
lurk just beneath the skin.

— 17 year-old girl

Emaciated Beauty

Pale skin and bare bones
A true image of beauty
Sunken face and thin wrists
A work of art before me
Hunger pains and dizziness
Replace the void inside me
Strip the fat and leave the bones
Reveal my inner beauty
Clarity of body and soul
Without the pain of food
Nourishment becomes enemy
The scale controls my mood
To eat is a sign of weakness
Restricting makes me whole
Emaciated beauty
Is the lining of my soul

— 14 year-old girl

Skeletons

I dreamt of yawning skeletons in my bed,
their bones clattering and clicking in their old joints,
teeth grinding together in their hollow skulls,
their bones bleached white from the desert sun.

They pressed against my body yearning for their
own missing flesh.
Their non-existent stomachs urged me
to press my own against my spine,
trying to trace my own bones in their place and
hide my living flesh.

I asked if I could become
hollow, delicate beauty as they were.
Their gaping eye sockets shook sadly with the remembrance
of their beautiful selves that once lived,
before ravens and crows covered their purple bruised flesh,
sunken valleys where curves of tissue should have been.

Their own self-torture produced empty spaces.
Painful to live, but addicting to nourish their worn images,
their bodies slipping through their hands like water,
never caressed by their accomplishments.

If they could have cried tears they would have.
Pressing me down, covering me with their bones,
they held my body, trying to remember the feeling of skin
roughened from the sun, warm from sleep.

They crooned in their mournful way,
singing of treasuring something before it's gone.
I ran my fingers over the curve of their skulls,
across their cheekbones and over their shoulders,
sliding my fingers down their ribs.

I could not help but wish for my own bones to show through,
as if I didn't have my own skin.
Yet they wished to have their own skin back,
wishing they had not tried to dig their graves with their fingers.

They kissed my flesh reverently, worshipping their own loss.
Their roughened bones scraped painfully against my skin.
I wished to wake up from my dream where my skin would not
hurt me
and I
would not wish for my own death.

— 16 year-old girl

These Shaky Hands

These shaky hands can't take much more.
Deprived from nourishment,
From self love,
Self acceptance.

Lightening hits my brain whenever rational thoughts appear.
Willie Wonka stands in front of you, waving a golden ticket in your face,
"Receive this as a prize,
but eat the chocolate that comes with it, and you're further away from it."

I am trapped in a well.
These walls are slippery,
And I am desperate to reach the top.
I'm so far away, but can feel the warmth of light on the top as I reach my hand closer…

This disease is so selfish.
Only thinking about two things,
The goal,
The numbers.

I let her define me as a person with these tools.
A number is what makes me myself?
Something as simple as weight?

No wonder these hands are trembling,
These eyes are bloodshot,
Vertigo hits me every time I stand up.

I've made myself believe that thin is a skill,
That starving is an excellent example of willpower.
Like a grandfather clock, my brain has been set to believe these things.
I am programmed, much like a robot.

I am listening to someone that is taking me away from the ones I love most.
Because of her selfish needs,
Because of my fear of food,
Of judgment.

The ideas spread like wildfire in my mind,
The planning of the rest of my life begins.
I am dismantling myself, my very soul, my inner core,
For something that is so materialistic.

I am a victim of myself,
My own thoughts,
My own self protection.
I am my greatest enemy, and yet my best friend.

Recovery is the most bittersweet delicacy I've had.

—15 year-old girl

My Story

The yelling.

The fighting.

The arguing.

It was all I used to hear.

Almost everyday I would go home and hear the fighting, to the point that I would go off into my own world, blasting music so I wouldn't hear the voices from downstairs.

It didn't help that I was not doing well in school.

When my report card came home the arguing and the anger would be turned onto me.

But soon it would go back to "How are we going to pay for this?"

or

"Why do we need to do this?"

While all this arguing was going on, I would try to stop it,

try to show them it wasn't just them that this arguing was affecting.

I tried telling them to stop. I tried running away.

Finally only one thing came to mind.

Suicide.

Thankfully though, my mind saved itself with one statement to my father.

"Dad, hide my rifle."

…

What he said to me changed my mindset.
He prevented me from carrying out my plan.
"Don't even think like that. You have too much going
for yourself."
With those 12 words he saved my life and to this day he is the one I go to for help.

— 17 year-old boy

Suicide

Every person entitled to life
Some brought down by strife
Without thought, opportunities are gone
Their body is suddenly withdrawn
No longer with the ones they love
Never told they were a soaring dove
Negativity is what brought them down
Without someone to talk to this causes them to drown
Drown in deep water, even more in shallow
No one knows their pain because they kept it in the shadow
Dark in the corner, even dark in the light
Their smile and conversation can't clue you in to their plight
Think it wrong or think it right
How do you get so desperate to make it forever night?
Those left behind have to work through the smoke
You may think life is hard
But for some living it is no joke

— 16 year-old boy

Mother and Daughter

i. Mother

Sit down child,
And I'm going to tell you how it is.

I am your mother. You are the daughter.
Got it?

You listen when I speak,
I am the truth.

You're a slut. Hoe. Way too much skin.
Don't dress like that anymore.

That music you listen to?
I HATE it.
Don't play it anymore.
My music is better.

Shut up and listen.
Don't you DARE walk away.
I am not done with you yet.

Those grades? Much too low.
You didn't work hard enough.

The book? Why are you reading it,
Talk to me instead. I am your world.

YOU want to go OUT?
Fine.

Only if you can get your OWN ride.
I WON'T take you.

Later. Ask me later. Maybe I'll have an answer …
or I'll forget
causing you to lose one more moment to be by yourself.
You are not you and you can't be without me.
You only hate me because I am you.
I'm not holding you back with chains. Go ahead.
TRY to fly away with your underdeveloped wings.
You don't have the experience to escape.
All you can do is burn.
You are mine.
Always.

ii. Daughter

Who… who am I?
I can't tell you who I am.

How annoying, when you ask me

"What do you want to do?"

What ever you do.

"What do you want to do?"

Anything. You can choose.

"Why don't you?"

Really, I don't mind.

"I want you to choose."

Really? Me? Choose?
I want… I want…. to see a movie.

"Which one? I don't mind at all."

Are you sure? I don't want to pick something-

"I won't like? Don't worry.
It's your turn to pick."

I think…possibly…an action? No, Star Wars.

> "Perfect. I'd love to too."

I chose. I made a choice? See,
> I can spread my wings.

Thank you.

> "You're welcome.
> You can always choose."

Thank you.
For that moment.
For letting me find myself.

How odd that sensation was.
It started in my stomach, the butterflies of fear, then…
the warmth in my chest.
Not…fear, but wanting to make the choice
as it rumbled up my throat,
buzzed through my brain,
and back out my mouth.
Thank you,
For breaking the chains and starting me on the path,
but not showing me the way.

That's my choice.
Always.

15 year-old girl

Complete the 360

You tell me that you have nothing,
That no one cares.
You tell me you have no one at all.
Do you see what is around you?
Do you realize that people are worse off than you?
Open your eyes.
You tell me that happiness isn't worth working for,
That it is just a waste of time.
You tell me it is easier not to be the nice person.
Let me show you the person you used to be.
Let me show you the person who made me smile.
Open your eyes.
Look at how much you have changed for the worse.
Turn yourself back around and complete the 360.
Make your change for the better.
Do you hear what I am telling you?
Do you see what lies beneath your frustration?
Open your eyes.
You have people that care about you and love you.
You have a life worth living.
You deserve to be happy.
Open your eyes.

— 15 year-old boy

We Are Light

It is the dark that illuminates
and the candlelight takes away the dark.
Although we enter winter, each day gains light.
Light is that which we need to survive,
light from within, as well as without.
Light from within, which shines out who we are.
We are light.
And all this time, I've been waiting for what I already have.

— collaborative poem by adult women

Confronting You

do you enjoy bringing me down
making me cry
making me frown
making me drown in my own tears
making me paranoid
making me fear
hurting me in such a way
that I really don't want to live another day
leaving me alone when you're supposed to take care of me
messing with my mind
needing therapy
making it hard for me to trust anyone
ruining my life
thinking it's fun
you lost my love when you took yours away
yet I told you I loved you yesterday
but I guess that's what happens when you're scared to try
get all bottled up, then you start to lie
get all emotional
and then wonder why
your heart starts to break
and then just dies.
why don't you understand that you're making me sad?
this poem is for the love I never really had.

— 15 year-old girl

Grab Your Life and Run

I watch it happen day by day
There is never any affection
Never any love

He throws you around
He's just pulling you down

You watch the clock
You want to leave

You can't
Your life is in the corner

Thinking of her you stay
What's life without a mom and dad together

There's no love, just lust
You're just a punching bag
A stress reliever

The clock is moving slower and slower
He is coming home later and later
Grab your life and run

— 16 year-old boy

Full of Love

I am beautiful, strong, and independent,
as I stand alone in the middle of a field.
I look around me, loving every beautiful creature I see.
Then I look at myself and realize that I really am beautiful.
I love all that is around me and all that is me.
I listen to the wind and I gently begin to sway gracefully.
It's like I am dancing to music and all creatures watch me.
I am one with myself and I love myself for that.
As the seasons change I don't change. I'm still the same.
I can feel the sun on me, warming me up and making me smile.
As I listen to the water in a brook rolling by, I'm relaxed.
When dark, gray clouds roll by, I cry and don't know why,
but all this time I know in my heart what being happy is.
For me, happiness is all this and so much more.
That is why I am me.
That is why I am truly beautiful.
Yes, I have ugly flaws, but we all do, everyone,
that is what makes me unique
and that is what makes my heart so full of love,
not just for myself, but for everyone, even people I do not know.

— 30 year-old woman

Were You Thinking About Me?

Memory
The day we sat and talked for hours, you wiped the tears from my eyes, your hand gentle, resting on my neck. I know you were thinking about me then.

Reality
But what about the time you went to light up, knowing I was waiting for your call, so I knew you were alright. Were you thinking about me then?

Memory
Watching football, talking about the most random things, just you and me. I know you were thinking about me then.

Reality
When you showed up at the dance, high. You knew I had been waiting for that night, yet you said the drugs were so alluring. Were you thinking about me then?

The Truth
It's back and forth
Good and bad
Happy and sad
But the disappointment has become too much
I can't stay here anymore
I need to let you go
I'm letting you go
Right now I'm thinking about you
Now and forever I'm thinking about you
And for you

I'm leaving
I'm leaving to help you

I thought maybe if I left you, you would begin to realize how bad your problem is. I thought maybe you'd realize how badly you are hurting me, your niece, your friends, everyone.

— *collaborative poem by 15 year-old girls*

It's going to be cold this winter (so they say)

It's going to be cold this winter
and we'll remember this moment
and it will feel dream-like.
Maybe the warmth will stay with us.
I'll remember
the autumn poem created in the sun,
the blinding radiance I've been looking for.
Short green grass shivering in the wind,
our toes grip the Earth
with our blue sky backdrop,
the random whinny of a horse,
perhaps feeling left out?

The singing pine
The singing pine
The cricket's chorus
It is a prayer of joy
For this is no ordinary day
Our dance of communion
Brings us home...

— collaborative poem by adult women in a SafeArt retreat

Watch

The silver of my watch, shiny and reflecting the purple velour cuff so close to it,
Hangs loosely off my right wrist, blue mother-of-pearl face,
Little hand at seven, big hand at sixteen, seconds ticking by with a long, skinny line…
It keeps going and going, infinitely, yet it stops and seems to slow,
Black-strap molasses oozing off a spoon,
Slow like the second you realize your life has changed forever.

Freeze-frame, a picture snapped,
My mental photo album is full of them,
Seconds, mere moments,
When paths convened and strayed,
Criss-crossed and stopped at dead ends…

When I opened my mailbox and discovered another existence, another life inside,
Trying not to slip on the uphill ice, squinting from the sun's glare,
I hurried back inside, up my wooden stairs, and ripped it open, confused,
Not recognizing the return address.
And later I read in disbelief as the support and the person unfolded from inside
And I felt struck as if by lightning, flabbergasted, electrified.
One moment, one second, crossroad…

Or when I saw him, only 18, wave goodbye on his bike,
Off into the June Indiana pink morning,
Balmy, corn fields in the distance, no more school!

Blonde curls, unmoving, hangover apparent as the bike swayed, smiling to me.
Our own little secret and the promise of more,
Only to find out later, that very night, he toppled over
Out the back of the pick-up, Cooper driving 65,
No streetlights on a flat back road,
Beer thickening their blood at ten p.m., screams as skull cracked
On the newly tarred road, friends jumping out of the now-stopped truck.
Dead end…

Walking home too late from work, 3 a.m. and ticking…
Only 16, long brown hair, no make-up, petite size two,
Stride to stride with the older one,
She liked him, had a crush…
She worked with him at the restaurant, taking orders in the front
As he cooked in the back, flirting and teasing.
She thought he really "liked her"…she didn't know any better.
But he was 20, Mother would not approve.
He had short blonde hair and a slight build, lots of friends.
She thought he was cute…
As they approached the mini-brook, brisk night air chilling her core,
He kissed her and she warmed…
But then his tongue turned slimy, groping, probing,
like a serpent.
He twisted around her, constricted her, pushed her down, and forced her,
Ripping at the plain clothes, blades of dewy grass on the exposed skin.
She glanced over and noticed a tiny drop of condensation on a green blade
Next to her eye, felt a small jagged rock scraping repeatedly across her back…

She looked back and kept saying no, held down by tentacles,
Scared to scream, of alarming the elderly couple that lived
in the house,
Attached to the lawn, adjacent to the mini-brook.
He kept going, turning into a strange, grunting,
squinty-eyed beast, as she cried,
tears joining the dew on the grass, in searing pain, ripped in half.
She finally stopped fighting and gave up...
And in that moment, she escaped her body, went numb,
lost her power,
Raped of her innocence, just a second...

My silver watch still hangs, coldly reflecting,
An observer to the life around it...
No opinions, no judgments, just facts.
The big and little hands keep circling around the blue mother-of-pearl face,
And the long silver line continues to tick away the seconds...

— 25 year-old woman, while in prison

Emptiness

Who is this who stands beside me?
Who's always next to me, behind me?
Who drags me down when times are tough?
Who copies my every move
To mock me and make fun of me?
Who cries the same tears?
Who is always there, but still I feel alone?

At first I am polite, and smile.
Then I get the courage to speak up
And say, "Hey…how's it goin'?"
She doesn't say anything back,
She just looks at me.

I'm so confused, she looks so familiar…
But I can't put my finger on it.
Who is she?

How dare she not answer!
I was nice to her, trying to make her feel comfortable,
Comfortable enough to say something.
Does she not care what people think?
Or is she so scared that at the thought of her speaking,
Not a single word comes out?
Whatever it may be, I just stare straight at her
Saying under my tongue,
"Hey, don't sweat it, I can relate to you, I've been there before."
I want to say that to her.
I go to open my mouth, about to say what's on my mind…
Nothing comes out.
I move to the side and switch position…

She does the same.
I stop suddenly, like a cat ready to pounce on its prey.
She doesn't move either.
Who is this in front of me?
Who's looking right at me??

That's it. I've had it.
My mind blacks out
With all the anger and frustration.
I make a fist and strike.
Now as I sit in the corner, looking at the blood in shock…
I glance down at what once was the mirror hanging on the wall.
I see her…
It was me.

— 16 year-old girl

Forever Time

The wind swirled and whipped and blew me away,
Off my feet, away from my soul.

In a dark place,
Dark, save for jagged streaks of lightning.

Could it ever stop? Stop? Stop?

Slowly, slowly, slowly, the wind died down.
The slow forever time began.
When nothing mattered, nor did I know where I was.
Where had I been, where? And when? And why?

Then everything became still…still and frozen in that forever time.

Slowly again, but slightly.
Slightly again, but slowly…a gentle breeze began.
A breeze to gather me together again.
Warm, sweet, heavenly air
drawing me in with it toward the future and the light.

— 45 year-old woman

Where it All Ends

She gets home about 8:30
and he's waiting at the door.
She knew what was coming
even before she hit the floor.
How long will she wait?
How much more can she take?
He promised her the world,
but that's hardly what he gave her.
Her black eyes and hidden bruises
remain secrets concealed
by make-up and dark glasses.
She's gotten good at hiding them
and nobody ever seems to notice.

But tonight she's decided
that it's her last night of hiding.
The secrets will become revealed.
The cards are on the table.
It's over, he won't touch her again.
It's over, that's where it all ends.

— 16 year-old girl

I Can Get a Grip

The lights of my room begin to fade away
and my brain looks back on recent days.
I can't look into his eyes without fear.
Will his brain finally become clear?

Chorus:
Just ignore the bruises on my face.
It's not your fault that I'm out of place.
I can taste the blood from my lip.
I'm really fine. I can get a grip.

I get good grades at school
and yet he calls me a fool.
Every night I wonder to myself,
Will my body be broken on the shelf?

Chorus:
Just ignore the bruises on my face.
It's not your fault that I'm out of place.
I can taste the blood from my lip.
I'm really fine. I can get a grip.

He yells and screams in my face,
tells me, "Get out of my place!
You no longer belong here.
Don't fuck with me boy, show me fear."

Chorus:
Just ignore the bruises on my face.
It's not your fault that I'm out of place.
I can taste the blood from my lip.
I'm really fine. I can get a grip.

I tell him he needs to get help
for he makes me and my mother yelp.
Maybe now he will finally see
the pain he's caused inside of me.

I won't ignore the bruises no longer
for I want to help my father.
Won't you see that you must do the same
in order to keep your family sane.

— 18 year-old man, song lyrics

As One Moment Passes

I wonder when it happened,
the exact moment.
What was the reason?
Was there anyone to talk to?

I just can't grasp
how important that one moment was,
to me, to my life, my future.

My whole life feels like a domino effect,
starting with that one moment
many years ago,
before I was even born.

I find the emotional pain
harder to handle
than the physical.
It lasts longer,
hurts deeper.

We try not to talk about it,
about him.
I guess it hurts everyone too much.
I hate.
I'm in a rage.
Angry.

As a child I didn't understand.
It's not that I couldn't,
I just didn't want to.

Nobody could make me believe the truth.
The words would come out of their mouths
and pass over my head.
I wouldn't believe it.

But the pain of it all hurt too much,
with no one to blame but myself.
So I had to lash out.
I had to get angry.
I had to believe the truth of it all.

There have been so many years
that I've wasted away,
so many people I let slip away.
I was too afraid to live.
I've come to realize that
I shouldn't be ashamed.
It wasn't my fault.
It isn't my fault.

My father is an alcoholic.
He's a deadbeat alcoholic.

I wonder when it happened,
the exact moment.
What was the reason
for him to pour that bottle down his throat?

I wonder if it hurts him
to realize that he failed us.
Does he realize?
Was that bottle worth his family and friends?

What was his reason?
Was there anyone to talk to?

— 18 year-old woman

Alcoholic

Alcohol abuse is a
Lack of self control,
Causing
Overheated arguments that
Happen to lose control.
Over a period of time,
Loved ones start to disappear
Into the darkened nights.
Children huddle in fear.

— 14 year-old girl

The Man Behind the Bottle

Substance abuse of any kind, not only messed with the abuser's mind.
Family and friends are affected by this, and they fix it with a metaphoric kiss.
Constant drinking and fighting, their sober selves constantly hiding.
Whether we're close or far apart, him stopping to drink will never start.
Crying and fighting, we have to deal.
Our inside wounds will never heal.
Promises are always broken.
Lies they tell are never spoken.
They're nice and fun when they're good and done.
Until it starts again the next day, and we end up feeling the same way…

— *collaborative poem by two 15 year-old boys*

Smoke Rings

Silently staring,
eyes scanning the room ever so
carefully,
he slowly eases back into the chair,
still cautiously
waiting.
The room stares back,
his family squinting their eyes,
smiling through their gritted teeth.
His youngest daughter gets up and walks
towards him.
She bends down to kiss
his balding head goodnight,
while his rings of smoke
rise in the air like poison,
suffocating his family,
killing him,
only to leave the ghosts
of the smoke rings behind.

— 16 year-old girl

The Secret

When I sit here and THINK about it,
It doesn't hurt.
When I TALK or HEAR about it, it kills me.
I've tried to hide it,
But I never succeed
I try to run away from it
But it always finds me,
How do I cope? When I seem to be ruined
And I can't trust anyone
Function is something I no longer know
How to do
When it comes down to intimacy
Why did my mom ever run into you?
You destroyed my family. You tore me apart
I kept it a secret because I THOUGHT
My mom was happy…
Until I heard that you hit her and hurt her as well…
Once we were all safe, (my brother, mother and me)
I told my mom how you touched me, hit me,
Starved me, scarred me…
And now as I get older, wiser and stronger
I sit in the woods, listening to the water rushing by
As it takes your voice inside my head away,
When the wind blows it takes my thoughts along with its course
The smell of you is covered by the smell of spring,
And you thought you could control me?
Sorry, but I'm not going to let you win.
And now I am Older, Wiser AND Stronger

—16 year-old girl

Back Rooms

Sweep it under the rug
Forget about the past
They don't realize I'm in the dust
I'm the one they've cast
Those hands weren't mine
Remember that face
They took away something
No one can replace
  Scream it
  Plead it
  I'm no longer whole
 Believe me
  Save me
  Those hands broke me
  They broke me
My hero seems meaningless
But now that he's gone
It shouldn't be forgotten
Even though it's been so long
The truth hurts more now
My body was defenseless
They changed my mind
I still can't trust the fences
  Scream it
  Plead it
  I'm no longer whole
 Believe me
  Save me
  Those hands broke me
  They broke me
Choking up on those words

But she had to go on
So much of the truth
Makes me wish she were wrong
They used me for a pleasure
That caused too much pain
They screwed up my world
I can never be the same
    Scream it
    Plead it
    I'm no longer whole
  Believe me
    Save me
    Those hands broke me
    They broke me
Don't sweep it away
The words were still spoken
    Scream it
    Plead it
    I was broken.

— 16 year-old girl

On the Shoulders of Many

"It's not my fault."
She knows it not.
She thinks to herself,
"They all know.
They hate me for it.
They know it's my fault."

She does anything to end the pain,
The suffering, the feeling of loneliness.
When she sees her blood pooling,
Dripping down her arms,
She is better,
But the pain is not sated.

She pulls away,
Unaware that they are pulling closer,
Seeing the despair in her eyes.
She is unable to speak of the incident,
The night she first saw him,
The shadow of torment he wore as a cape.

That night plays over and over in her head,
The uncertainties of it a constant question.
Did he have protection?
Did I say no?
She is locked in a dark cage,
Unable to escape the fear and uncertainty.

She did not know.
Over 64,000 people were in the same boat,
1 person every 2.5 minutes,

What would people think?
How would they react?
Nobody can know.

That's when she saw him,
His cape wreaking havoc amidst the crowd.
She felt incapable of feeling.
It was then she realized she must tell.
This was a bomb inside her ready to explode,
Explode and tear him down.

He wouldn't do this again.
He would not go unpunished.
Strangled by his own cape,
Unable to do more harm,
Realizing by stopping him she would be free,
She would be out of the darkness.

That was when she told the injustice of that night,
So long ago,
How he raped her,
Used her,
Made her feel like nothing,
How he had destroyed her spirit.

What she thought would happen never did,
The blame, the gossip, the whispers.
She was surrounded.
It was then she realized she was not alone,
But on the shoulders of many,
Holding her up and supporting her.

— 16 year-old girl

Warm Me, Warm Me

Warm me, warm me as I wander,
Warm me as I walk.
I seek a peace not easily found,
As I search the Earth around.
Sun and Moon and Stars are my friends,
They watch me ere I go
And every lesson I've ever learned
They already know…

Warm me, warm me as I wander,
Warm me as I walk.
I seek a truth not easily found,
As I search the Earth around.
A friend is gone, not to return,
Not as the woman I knew.
Her spirit is free to flow around me
And I know that's exactly what she'll do.

Warm me, warm me as I wander,
Warm me as I walk.
I seek a justice not to be found,
As I search the Earth around.
My mother said when I was a child,
Life isn't always fair.
Certain things you have to accept,
Although the pain is hard to bear.

Warm me, warm me as I wander,
Warm me as I walk.
I seek a love not easily found,
As I search the Earth around.

Lessons learned include grief and anger,
Equal parts joy and mirth,
And peace, truth, love may be found, in death as well as birth.

Warm me, warm me as I wander,
Warm me as I walk.
I found the peace, I found the truth, I found the love
Not easily found, as I searched the Earth around,
As I searched the Earth around.

Song by Tracy Penfield, in memory of Carol

Acknowledgements

Having worked personally with hundreds of *SafeArt* workshop participants over the past decade, reading each piece conjures for me the memory of a voice, a face, a person becoming whole. I am grateful to them for their honesty and bravery and, most of all, their trust. For someone who has been abused, this is perhaps the most challenging factor in forming relationships with anyone: learning to trust. I thank them for not only sharing their stories in our established groups, but for being willing to put them out in the world. They recognize the need to speak out for themselves and on the behalf of others.

Reading through ten years of writings was a monumental task, and I deeply thank my co-editor and *SafeArt* colleague Josey Hastings for her ability to be objective and unerring in her focus on tuning this collection to a fine pitch. We then had many eyes and hearts involved in the final readings, and we thank you all: Caro, Chelsea Rose, Carl, Jennie, Mary Jean, Wynona, Emily, and the *SafeArt* Healing Arts for Women Group.

Finally, I want to express my gratitude to Chip Norton and the Kristy Norton Memorial Fund, which has helped to finance the creation of *On Our Way...* Chip's daughter Kristy, a believer in the healing arts, wrote, "It is only in difficult places that we search for inner peace, and it is in difficult places when peace matters most." Thank you, Chip, for realizing the importance of the Anthology, and then helping us to manifest it.

Tracy Penfield